AF268950

Year of Valentines
John Reed

SPUYTEN DUYVIL

New York City

Late

Where were you driving? A few nights ago.
With your knuckles at the top of the wheel
and your arms braced like you were holding up
the front end of, hmm, was it a sedan?
Was it very late? I think so.
You'd expected to be there already
and hunched into your headlights on the road,
which snaked onto nowhere between the trees.
You drove like the table was set for you
and dear friends were candlelit and waiting.
And you turned the dial on the radio
and forgot my eyeball, still in your heart
(blood, saline) blinking behind your aorta.

Pointe Shoes

The birds know what you're up to but don't tell. And the trains I take are rerouted to you as soon as I get off and the doors close. And people are always talking to you, on the phone or over coffee or drinks, right before and after they talk to me. You're looking up in the covered well; and you're out there, whirligigging pointe shoes—adorning cable lines at roundabouts. I know. I know you're finding lost kittens where the suburb ends with Industry Road; and you're the cabin cook of Two Valleys; and the spirit that speaks through every bell.

Everywhere But Here

You and I are everywhere but here.
Down on Gansevoort at the swanky bar,
the cherrystone clams are ready for us,
on ice on a platter, on the half shell—
and the sprinklers time-on at the great lawn—
and an orange skirt is somewhere walking—
and drivers are adjusting their mirrors.
We're 24/7, below Canal,
in the alterverse where the lights stay on,
the shutters stay up, the phone keeps ringing,
and "they" are bones like snowdrifts in corners.
We're orphaned only in this universe,
but there, we're in my chest and in your ha8r.

Party Tricks

You really had all the best party tricks.
Like that time you pulled me into a hat.
Nevermind the delight when I climbed out.
And what a fantabulous cabinet
of curiosities. That one display.
Not only the prince pauper, rag and bone,
but a perfect twin in the pauper prince,
shoes and watch and a better bicyclette,
and just as broken and shining a trophy.
You, with your baton and ringmaster tails,
standing at the top of the stairs, Pinot
Noir and another walk-up sublet,
and candy bowls filled with wooden matches.

Knife Fight

Do you remember when we couldn't sleep?
So we got up and got dressed and went out
into the city of others and lights,
and I took the C and you took the 7,
and we hadn't been talking and had no
plan or prearranged place to rendezvous
but we met in Times Square, amidst the ghosts
of suicides, who carried shopping bags
with their lives in them. And in the station,
we got the A train and had a knife fight,
and rolled around in one of those new cars
with saucy gyro wrappers on the floor—
and we cut ourselves to shreds, and bled out,
and I forgot you, and you forgot me.

But Don't

But don't send a photo of a wine glass
just swirled, les larmes de vin, with Pinot Noir.
And don't beckon and dance in a tank top
woven in white and Playa Venao.
And don't thread your hand in your hair and hide
your face, as if I shouldn't be looking,
as if I could forget how now I'm half.
And don't promise we'd go blind for an hour
with sun or snow or moonshine or A-bombs.
And don't tell stories of the Coast Starlight,
or little old houses in Brittany.
And please don't say tomorrow, tomorrow.
And don't airkiss me or whisper-witch "yes."

Your Name Was Written All Over Me

We were there on the streetcorner,
standing too close together, or too far apart,
and your name was written all over me,
in fat marker, chisel-tip, red and black.
Oh, and all caps. Name, first and last, and times
and dates, and percentages, usually
quite high, like eighty-eight or ninety-four.
The red ink had wept onto my collar,
and that friend of yours, or maybe mine,
looked from you to me, and from me to you,
while we acted like sorta acquaintances,
making introductions, nonchalantly—
until our witness fled. Run in a walk, and zipping up
[whose friend?] for (plausible) deniability.

Road Kill

But the birds have no graves, my love, once love,
and there is heaven there, where they reside—
where these feathers are still green, red, still gold.
Is it heaven, darling, heaven, where we've gone?
Heaven darling, I do I do I do,
if we are ahead, anyway, I do.
If, my darling—but don't write back—I do.
Darling, light no fires, these wings still luff.
But who? Who then, darling, if we are not?
But who then darling, who, would still have eyes?
But who then darling, who, will name the roads?
Who then, darling, will shiver with the doves?
Dearest, darling, my once love, and who will rove?

Ten Years

You know ten years don't matter to me,
that when you drew your too-sharp fingernail
across the black nylon, I'd still be here,
saying we just danced—didn't we just dance?—
trying to pull your forearm through the hole,
trying to get my head through just one drink,
just one drink, wherever you want to meet,
because you know, you and I, you know.
We don't weep, and the sky falls when we blink.
In this life, there are some kinds of orphans,
who lie in the depth of this very well.
You and I, we know there are no stars.
You and I, we've come to the hour agreed.

kapOW :)

I sat there at the window a long time,
watching the people—up and down Broadway.
They came in all kinds, but you know I liked
the charming, brilliant, beautiful ones—
charming being not only the first part
but the better part of the other parts.
(Ha) I'd laugh when I saw the real Red Hots
hurry by—kapOW!—only to ignite,
burn thrusters, and, WHOOSH, rocket GAH-gone.
Jet-fueled by talent and St. Patrick's Day,
and loved ones and, I guess, souls, etc. :)
(Haha, I laugh now) how you were so bright
and I should have known (ha) from jump (haha)
how you'd come crashing through the glass in flames.

Cloth Monkey Make Me Jumpy

Cloth monkey, say you're sorry. Say you are.
Cloth monkey, smother me in fuzzy pile.
Cloth monkey, tsk and pshaw Vallée de la Loire.
Cloth monkey, I can worry like a child.
Cloth monkey, give me cookies—crisp and rummy.
Cloth monkey, make me jumpy. Stick your tongue out.
Cloth monkey, weep me—on your terry tummy.
Cloth monkey, do-no-harm me when I'm seven.
Cloth monkey, come with ice and pour me twice.
Cloth monkey, peel me roses—with becauses.
Cloth monkey, itemize me—any price.
Cloth monkey, sing me sudsy lullabies.
Cloth monkey, knead you, knead you—with my claws.

Spring Cleaning

For spring cleaning, you should come over here,
and after we're done I'll go over there,
and after that we'll head to the city,
and then take the highway to the suburbs,
and then find the dirt road to the country,
and hop a helicopter to the Pole;
and we'll toss the old file cards and cheap beer,
and clean out the desk and the Frigidaire,
and push trash bags of stuff out the window,
and fill the dumps with hard drives and CDs,
and gather papers and passports to burn,
and buff hearts & arrows off big, barked trees,
and seal the bodies in virgin barrels,
and roll them to the piers and the quarries.

"K"

What if I say you're fine, spelled with a K?
What if you said nice? K N I C E.
What if we had glitter eyes and wood hands?
And what if the curtain dropped again?
And we were unstoried, unseen, unheard,
and unbelieving of the other sides—
l8ve, d8th, all the way to the balcony.
No puppet maestro two-handing the stage,
no footlights to set our flounces aflame,
no crying crescendoes or brassy bands,
no love-me, love-me-nots. (Spelled with a K.)
What then? Is the audience enraptured?
Or felted and velveteen, quicksand and lime.

Queen Mother

For three days, just three, I could see the strings:
the ones that come out of our hands and feet;
and the little eyehook ones on our necks;
and the top of the head ones, and chin ones—
and the ones people have to work their waists.
I could see how the strings went taut, pulled first,
and how all of us were about to spin.
We had newly glued clothes, joints fixed with tacks,
mitten fingers, and fresh heads in paste
with papier-mâché eyes, painted to weep.
The poor souls with no jaw-hinges nodded, lips pursed,
while the rest of us yawped: of crops and kings;
and our queen mother, who let us eat cake.

Heads and Haha

Our puppet heads are wooden, but heavy,
no good for kissing, but better for trying.
If you would remember my puppet name,
I could be an as-if someone again,
clattering promises you would ask for. If,
if we kissed, would we kiss with open mouths?
I don't think I have a hinge in my jaw;
I think my mouth is carved in a pucker,
maybe shaping a word that can't be said,
or tasting the wish by licking the flame.
If your face is carved like mine, with no hinge,
our wooden heads will peck please, please, please.
But if, if we have hinges and chins? Who
would we be to toss our heads and haha?

Strings on the Sparrows

I should have said the first strings were my own.
I was thinking of you, maybe. Maybe
I was thinking of you thinking of me,
when I saw a loose knot in my palm, slack
before it went taut. All my strings
went taut. That's how I found the six others.
Each string is blue and white, baker's twine,
but really old: frayed, dirty and yellow.
I thought it was a curse on once lovers,
that it was that "no, there is no nothing,"
but then I saw the strings of the redcap
who drove the baggage through the empty station,
in a cart that had its own set of lines,
and outside, there were strings on the sparrows.

When the Puppet Master

19

I remember when the puppet master
sat at the same window in the same gray light,
with the same rolled glass panes of six and six,
and the same wood frame to nod yes or no,
and not-now laughed and turned back to the bench.
I remember the knots of your nine strings,
like weedflowers in childhood meadows,
and how each knot uncoiled, unwilling,
and you fell to a heap, pirouette spent.
And when my own strings went slack, to the bone,
I remember that we were limb to limb,
and that the master went out for the night,
and that our strings were tied to each other.

After This

So maybe after this Armageddon,
there really will be a resurrection,
and our souls will rise up from our bodies,
and we'll be set free from flesh and from d8th,
and be incarnated, much more durably,
and for longevity, in the patient,
waiting puppets, of which there are many,
that we've left behind—tucked in basinets,
sitting on wicker chairs in vestibules,
festooning branched hat racks on screened porches—
with their felt, glass, porcelain and bead eyes,
with their painted pupils, and pouting lips,
and their quiet prophesy of heaven.

So So

I don't think I'm ready to talk to you. I guess I could
be afraid of something—of "you," of "me," of "too
late," and "too soon," of words that write themselves
behind my eyes, on black slate, in chalk or maybe
gypsum. If it's fear, that's a weak word for the it that
threads with a bodkin into my abdomen and loops
back out. You know, that stitch that slings us into days
of disappointing gifts, and wet landings in unknown
diseases. If I'm afraid, I'm afraid of the future, of you
on the other end of these strings, so listless with your
yoke thé buffoons, and so so looking for something
else to do.

Hallways

Twenty years, knock knock, and I'm without strings,
while you, too, rattle your knobs down hallways.
If hawseholes still linger, I don't look for them.
I don't wonder, darling, about the hand,
which waits, without a palm, without an other—
no valence of clouds or eyes in the blue—
mantled above what we can remember,
above the de8d side and our varnished pupils.
But what if, what-if we, our cords untangled,
quivered by our fetters, ensnared again?
And the footlights kindle our wooden faces,
and we toss embraces to jointed limbs,
suspended, while we clatter painted lips.

A Long Night

A long night, my love, my sweet sick sunrise, my
drunken dawn, my pearly, priceless doom. Who
but you? Waiting in my blinking eyes, churning in
exhaustion—my reckless fume. Dirty feet, white
thighs and somebody's bride; divorcee, chapped lips
and laughter to lie for. We had no shame but we both
had our pride. Never were you mine, never was I
yours. Never came the nevermore, the sorrow for the
lost cold war, the bickered, battered bedroom sores,
mascara charred and marrow bored. I hate how they
knew we would shatter. And whoever invented the
promise had no love, made no concession, for us.

Meadow-bright

You lied to me about everything.
But I knew you were a special case.
You couldn't help yourself from pairing us,
we were so the same and so different:
two fine horrors, one ice and one water;
two bleeding darlings, sweeter and better.
And except at Pete's Candy, and Café
8, you were no queen, and we were no kings—
so why not build a castle of jam jars?
And so what, you got a little too much?
It was enough for Misters Wrong and Rent.
It was enough, and a bucket of tar—
and Meadow-Bright lies like poppies in spring.

LOL

I knew we'd be seeing each other again.
It looks like everyone else is here, too.
All of us, once angels, who finally finished falling.
We were so crazy about here and there,
when the little difference was "always,"
or the other eternity, "never."
Just listen to all of this childless laughter.
Now we are gone, and here we can stay,
you and I, who are you and I no more,
who tore apart our daughters for the bears,
who offered our sons to g8d, LOL,
who are, we know, we've forgotten who,
who are now outside of ourselves, without when.

Something S.

I was just minding my own business, just sitting around,
all by myself, waiting for something shitty to happen, when
you showed up again, waving, waving your long arm and
buttered toast fingertips, and asking if I miss you, which I
do, which I do, which I do, which I do, and then you left,
again, teeth without lips. Come over here, my doe-eyed
once darling, and kiss me when you do that. Kiss me when
you kick the bread crumbs and the pigeons laugh, when
you toss out your hands and make the sun. You, I do. Un-
der your sky, I do.

Brass Rings

And the tunnel of love at Love Canal.
When we were, what? Children? Pixies? Zombies?
The walking wounded? The last ones standing?
It was after the fires—Dreamland first—
but before we'd forgotten mermaids in
Adidas and the menu at Nathan's,
before the quiet of these petit mals.
Ten punches a ticket or two brass rings.
The midway prizes in three tries times three.
Under the boardwalk in Levolor sand.
Slushies and french fries in buckets and quarts.
Seagulls, saying, "never call, never call."
And the D train won't tell but sings and sings.

China Shop

Ok, you didn't need to break something. When people come into this china shop, they tiptoe around, they oo and they aa, and then when they walk out, they slam the door. I spend my whole life sweeping up the glass, rethreading crystals onto chandeliers, trying to Krazy Glue the porcelain, telling myself that it was just an accident, and I'll crawl around and find all the gears to reassemble the two grandfather clocks, which maybe needed cleaning, and then I'll fix the doorknob, which didn't even lock. Tomorrow, I can reattach the sign.

And Then

And then you were a fuzzywuzzy bunny.
And then you were a three-sided dagger.
And then you were a torn flag on a flagpole.
And then you were happy hour and nylons.
And then you were me, and then you were you.
And then you were a shack by a mountain.
And then you were a Billy Idol song.
And then you were Ziggy, then Jewel.
And then you were a June day with no fan.
And then you were money honey money.
And then you were a street and a stranger.
And then you were a red-check duffle coat.
And then you were here, and then you were g8ne.

Early & After

Can we meet very early one morning?
And I'll begin by asking a question
and you'll answer as you go about your
routine—change into a better t-shirt,
drink tea, check your feeds and pack your gym bag.
Maybe I'll walk with you in a meadow of
goldenrod, or a woods of wild ginseng.
Or maybe, in evening attire,
we'll go to the preview of La Bohème
and afterwards go to a Broadway bar,
and stay the course with the Prosecco from
intermezzo, and I'll listen and ask,
eye in eye, as you tell me everything.

Charge My Card

31

When I die, invite everyone over.
Make sure I'm stripped down, wherever I am,
there's no need to move me, or fix my face,
or take out my organs, or anything.
Just leave me like I am, just exactly
like I am: arms, hands, legs, feet, mouth, tongue, eyes.
No weapons—no boots, brass knuckles or swords—
barefoot is ok, as are elbow strikes,
but the fist, the closed fist, is mandatory.
Knee, heel, palm, forearm—but every third swing
is the fist, the fist until it stops or breaks.
Play music and serve blackberry brandy—
charge my card, and order in whatever.

13 Lies

The truth is, I only tell 13 lies.
Lie no. 2: I lie in praise of heaven.
3: this is between just the two of us.
4: in the silence we share, we are whole.
Yes, I heard you (5), I was listening.
Of course it matters to me. Very much.
No, it doesn't bother me, it's nothing.
Da-ding ... lucky cherries, ding, jackpot.
For every lie, I'll give you a nickel.
A lie is a live heart, hopping in dust.
Just a few minutes after 11.
You and I, we are a dozen goodbyes.
A better lie is a fountain of youth.
Without lies, none of us are beautiful.

I.O.U.

You owe me a kiss on a streetcorner.
You owe me a red bike in a matchbox.
You owe me hat porn and buttered scone porn.
You owe me a dozen wilted roses.
You owe me your cats. Any new ones, too.
You owe me six lies and one you told me.
You owe me a Suntory soda.
You owe me the best beach and the best beach rock.
You owe me a crumpled horn, all forlorn.
You owe me your worn and tattered blouses.
You owe me cicadas in every brood.
You owe me acorns as big, fluffy trees.
I owe you a little, but you owe me more.

Spell

If sorrow had no lover, the petals of roses would sing, and night would not heal the wound, and we would not blink our eyes, still, still, and breathe these ashes, these ashes, through our teeth. We would not melt the snow with our dreams, and water would not be wine with no color and no flavor, and the laughter of children, the other children, would not pierce the window, would not draw us so near the horizon. If sorrow has no lover, who will pour, and who will light the cigarette? And will there be no ivory blade to cut the seal? To read aloud the jinx? "I cast the spell."

Seven Blessings

Let's go somewhere, maybe take a taxi
to where the field meets the orchard in vines,
and we'll try to find where the blackberries,
who have no winter, cast blessings,
and the sky rides the locomotive,
whistling to you, whistling while the birds hush.
Come, and we'll steal the beekeeper's hive,
which hadn't he always intended for us?
Fruit crate hives in elevator buildings,
where the window glass is rolled of honey,
where we will tablecloth the linseed sun,
and pull out the benches and shed our keys,
and share equally between us one sky, once seen.

Ribbon & Bow

I've seen it, unexpectedly enough,
a few times, as I've hurried through my day,
hushed and losing things—everything really—
that I kinda had that inkling to keep.
Have you, from the window of your Uber,
ever caught a glimpse of the foil paper,
the need-me crimson ribbon with the ruffled bow?
I don't go back. No. But there it will be,
across the avenue, shining with rain.
Once I got super close, and touched the tape—
frayed, unstuck, like you'd also been "right here,"
not peeling back the tissue for a peek of
the gift that's addressed to the two of us.

Mi Mea (Culpa)

I kept a lock of your hair, which I used
to stuff the head of a doll I repaired,
which is here on my desk to pierce with pins
because aren't we friends? We'll always be
friends, friends to the end, hidey hidey ho,
my friend, sweet friend, who has no darts for me,
my friend, sweet friend, who won't hold up the phone,
so I can hear her breathe, mentiroso,
and exist in her follicles and spit,
and be there, just ahead, in her next chair, or
in a waiting thought, ripened by a bruise.
Por favor, un momento con mi amor,
sí, mi amor, mea memento mori.

Sunday Drive

It was a many layer chocolate cake with rum, berries and
I don't remember but everything, and only half eaten, and
you and I had as much as we could, given the late hour and
checkout time, given how drunk and full we were already,
given how much we still wanted to say. And should we
have cleaned the platter that night? (To see our futures
mirrored in silver.) Or was something better left untaken?
Crated and sent to the Rocky Mountains. So we could
Sunday drive suicide road and divvy the last slice, and
break the plates.

Hearts & Hands

Is that you again, standing next to me?
Wearing last night's dress, missing a button.
Rolling through the city like some big lie
moves the traffic this side of the freeway.
Wouldn't we be better off in three hours?
Wouldn't you have some of what you came for?
Aren't you looking ahead much too far?
These years come off with a drink and a shower,
and the choir observing a song of praise,
and hearts and hands living in defiance,
lifting the veils of our professions,
and drifting in the say-no-more of beasts,
défait, sauf pour le rire et le sommeil.

Be Mine

Be mine. Don't be friendly to other people.
Don't smile at all those other psychopaths.
I want you to drag your feet without me.
I want you to breathe like you're underwater.
I want you to die after each heartbeat.
I want you to feel bad about everything.
Except me. I want you to think of me.
Just me. Think of me as the sun and rain.
Think of me as the center of orbit,
and cold space as your innermost enemy.
Without me, go out and turn up your hat
and beg your betters to toss in nickels
that you scatter in skies sooted in diesel.

Four (Radiant) Children

When you were a girl, and I was a boy,
the trees had no kind, the doors had no #s,
and the wind did not carry the clatter
of bones, weathered and hollow, and once words.
Animals had our eyes, our short-life eyes,
and we knew the way to go in the sand,
and daylight was squeezed from lem8ns & limes,
and little lies were prey to little birds.
I lived within a prayer, when you were her.
And now we have North. We, we four, have North,
and to mourn, two weeks with the linden trees.
And when we're all together, the four children,
we're children without tongues, and without hands.

Nowhere

We were somewhere for something, then nowhere,
walking down an avenue in Brooklyn,
which appeared for you, amber and empty,
and going in the wrong direction,
away from my city that still loved me,
and into a borough with our shadows
painted in doorways, embracing in years.
Take me for ransom, and I'll make payment
with a cereal box full of centimes,
two Dixie cups attached by baker's twine,
and a living room set made of Lego.
My once flatterer, take me for ransom,
and I promise you my name, "désastre."

Says U:

43

"OK, wow, so that was unexpected.
I didn't mean to cut you, cut you,
with that razor, those razors,
and I know how you heal real quick,
and you're a machine, yes that you are,
and honesty is always best always,
but let's talk about a few other exes
of mine, who might serve as fine exemplars,
if you're feeling dumbstruck, or maybe sick,
or betrayed or tremendously alone,
and I mean really way tremendously,
like, lonesome as an orphan underwater
lonesome, like you wouldn't get what you'd get."

Never The Less

My mother danced late and never played chess.
She threw two hundred ravens at the doves.
One for every decade of the wars they forgave,
feathering the unconquerable sky.
My cousin chews the faces off wild dogs,
and laughs so hard at silly dreams they melt
like overdoses in silver soup spoons.
You were as loud as a Witch of the West,
beating hearts with mallets through fine mesh sieves.
Sí, mi amor, Krylon Coney Island.
Sí, mi amor, Frogger turtles and logs,
and crocodiles and cars and never tells.
Sí, mi amor, never and nevertheless.

Things Fall Off

Things fall off and roll under other things.

And sometimes they break when you're almost done.

And then you're late but you have to go back.

And people think they're being so clever.

And the cords are tangled just out of reach.

And what would we do without stubborn stains?

And what would we do with our precious time?

Maybe eat with our hands, much too loudly.

Maybe ask our frenemies for more money.

Maybe take the extra party favor.

Maybe flip the switches and hitch the latches.

And itemize what we can't leave behind.

And scream in tunnels on the sleeper train.

The (Dutiful) Fireman

I said I'd grow up to be a fireman.
And I knew it was something I could do.
At school, there were firemen on the posters
that were there to give you some safe ideas.
And there was a firehouse museum around
the corner, with steam fire engines, horsedrawn,
and old helmets, and axes and medals,
and photos of heroes, so many heroes.
Up winding stairs, in a garret theater,
the dutiful fireman would be stationed to
roll (for his one visitor) his one reel:
with crickets, matches, and sleeping smokers, and
infernos, however accidental—
that I just never wanted to put out.

The One

I know you'll be the one who comes for me,
and it shouldn't matter what you say now—
because ghosts have always been tapping me,
and they'll keep tapping for the forty years
of work I have left (if I'm lucky enough to work that long),
and you, they, and everybody knows,
that I've already risen from the ground
in silence, without horse hooves, rain, or snow.
You'll be the one, who in jest, I will hear,
as I once heard the seasons in the trees.
You will have your wings then, not just your bow—
and so what your darts, beneath a silent sea?
I know you're the one who will come for me.

The Mermaid Parade

Sea-moon blue. I marry the Paris sky (those eyes), and
a loose knit dress of fine wool. Just the color, and you
wonder why—our l8ve no more lie, our lives no less full
than a promise of pride or weeping want. The artist's
child will always miss the gulls, the thoughtless gaze, the
begging and the taunts—the lunar tides when Laight Street
is wet sand and the bayside town of seventeen-fifty-five and
buckets of beer and cherrystone clams, and poorhouses,
oysters, apples and dives. And l8ve is long or far between
us, the distance between New York and Paris.

Not Sorry

49

The things we've done. We'd laugh like angels
and say "I'm not sorry," every time.
And you'd wear prawn heads on your fingertips,
to promise forever, or wave toodle-oo,
or point to a crumbling Colliers atlas,
and foretell a destination with chairs.
And there'd be a prawn for every question,
for local knowledge or fixing the van—
to find dear friends and chèvres in nowheres.
Thrift jeans and plaid wool coats and La Pucelle,
and a neon sign and a bag of chips,
and hunters lodges with the same stairwell—
and deserts, and pink slips, and twists of lime.

Just Years

You leaned over the bar to arm wrestle.
You'd pulled me to a stool to let me win.
Red hair and green eyes and I lied and lied.
It was some other kid's birthday party,
but you weren't anybody's mother.
You had a tanned, freckled, sunburned bust,
and wore an Irish-rust, v-neck sweater,
and I said that no woman could beat me,
and boasted of other women who'd tried,
and you let me win again and again,
and made eyes when you felt my muscle,
and woo-wooed, part with love, part with disgust,
knowing that just years had come between us.

Coupon Booklet

I made you a seven coupon booklet.
I handwrote your name on the first coupon.
Over and over. It's good forever.
The second coupon is for a sweet cat.
The third one lets you pick a memory
to forget. (Crazy, crazy paperwork—
cities, states and nations—went into that.)
Coupon four, of course: a four-leaf clover.
Coupon five: a perpetuum place to sit.
For coupon six: two more days on the shore.
Seven: an only-for-you magic wand.
Your coupon booklet. Cold as cash money.
And all you have to do is come get it.

Creature Call

I'll form the word in my second heart,
which pumps perfume and presses on my lungs,
and your "hello" will arrive, a glass bird,
and swim-fly aorta to aorta,
and wait in my mouth, a hurt expectation
pressing—firm-bodied with oily young feathers
that taste of marjoram—to my lips, parted
(keep breathing) by the avulsion of you.
"Hello," cast to the city in autumn,
over Amsterdam and across the park,
over the reservoir and two museums—
over our streetlights, not seen and not heard.
"Hello," scheduled tonight for your Loch Ness.

Grabby

When you were a vampire in Pucci,
and I was a black rabbit on the town,
we danced for so long at the Guggenheim
that we lost our friends, and by accident
went to Vienna, where we turned into
dolls with cloth bodies and porcelain heads
(with expressions that could mean anything)
and were placed on a shelf for a lifetime,
staring at each other with repentance
until we were sincerely forgiven
and sent back, back to our Halloween bed,
to wake, to begin anew and atone—as if
there is sainting the undead, or bunnies.

"Author of All"

You got every single thing you wanted
by avoiding smiling liars like me.
You knew better than to trust those jackals,
with their arrow eyes and teeth like cold air,
with their laughter, their true-sounding laughter,
about lions who didn't make the kill.
"The lions," they'd say, "don't come until dawn,
long after the last child has been felled,
after the loin is stripped from the giraffe,
and fear cuts time and shows time to fear."
But Elizabeth, when your toast got dull,
and you needed someone to save you, needed
a hand to take the book, you turned to me. "John."

"John John"

55

"John John" automaton, born to never,
never learn. "John John" automaton, born
to never never learn. Born to ever
ever urn. Born to burn and born to scorn.
"John John" automaton, got nothing,
nothing, nothing done. "John John" automat,
nothing winning, always spinning spinning
spinning. John-a-folds his wrinkles flat.
"John John" automatic. Panic panic
panic panic. Needs to needs to needs to naught.
Needs machined, by house mechanic.
John-O-John, ought-to-John on auto ought.
Not John-o-ton. "John John" not John-o-ton.
"John John" not John-o-ton. "John John" not John ...

Nunjas

I'm only going to ask you for one thing.
From now on, I don't want to have a name.
When you see me, just say "Hey," or "Howdy,"
Or, "Oh, how lovely to see you this morning."
Don't say a word about the apostle,
who I was in the life before this one,
when Astor Place had a sky and no hotel,
and I was lithe and irritating,
with my dance moves and hopes and repartee
with my time for armies of killer nunjas.
From now on, don't talk of what I became.
From now on, talk to my eyes and my skin.
And no introductions. And don't call me "John."

One Condition

You said that maybe you could forgive me,
but first I had to get into the trunk
of the old Buick you meant to sell "soon."
And while I was in for a nine-hour drive
to the quarry at the end of the Earth,
I shouldn't be too uncomfortable
because you were ready with the injection,
if I'd be so kind and not cause trouble,
and "pretty please" cuff the sleeve of my shirt.
You suggested I curl up on my side—
never mind the shovels, there was lotsa room.
And here, gagged and zip-tied, the highway hums,
and you and I are you and me. Maybe.

Rubber Ball

Your rubber ball is somewhere in the closet.
Your rubber ball rolls from the tippy-top shelf,
bounces on/off the armoire, flees down the hall,
turns the corner at the gilded mirror,
and leaps over the sill—out the window,
into traffic, and through a yellow light.
You'd thought a quick check-up, and not much more,
and if just one bounce (if now was the time)
to take care, to visualize the fall day
when you would play hard, play to win—for trophies,
belts, and seals with your name in gold (embossed).
But your rubber ball hurdles two trucks,
takes the slot and the block and it's lost, lost, lost.

V & V

We'll cloak our bones for La Mascarada—
you in a crêpe gown and me in black muslin,
and all our v's and v's will pass through us:
ingress to egress, prayed-for sweet breezes;
torsos cleaned hollow by real mojitos;
echoes enchambered by años caprices;
vacant to capacity de nada.
Sí mi amor, and should we disrobe we'll
clack clavicles, interlace in thoraces,
bonk bonk mandibles, orbit to orbit,
and serpent our vertebrae in one den.
White stripes multiplied, distant Adidas.
Marathon 20s and O Superstars.

Short Shag

When you came down from your mountain village
looking for boys like me, the tragedies,
earthbound and heartsick and snarly as strays
(because that's what you liked, for no good reason)
you farewelled the wrong-headed, red-headed elves,
your family and friends of whatever
came before pixies, angels or demons,
whatever creature-beings, not quite para,
not quite terra, not quite venal or divine.
When you fell from grace on your avalanche,
you shed your spider-silk manteau at Goodwill,
and made the barber cut your hair, "short shag."
But you'll go back, you'll go home, when you're done.

"Your Name" & "Mine"

And when you found my gill, neck to navel,
and slipped in your head and whispered sweetly,
did you know the spell was impervious
to counter spells, charms or incantations?
Did you know without the words said and said,
your mouth and my chest would swell with "not full"
and the bitterend ashes of burnt lace?
Did you know? Did you know? Did you know then
what sorcery could be unspooled by three words?
Thrice to mine and thrice to thine. What bargain made?
What oath avowed like, "like, obviously"?
Just you and me in Hundred Acre Wood
with a treehouse and an "and" to our names.

Life Unweaved

You live on the other side of the world,
and somewhere between us, in the ocean,
me with my crutches and you with your curls,
and the green coffee house with big muffins,
and the fanciest restaurant in town
(that used fresh basil and canned tomatoes),
and you and me in s8x till we drowned,
and running through the corn to scare the crows—
we stay there, still and always wise young fools.
Bruised, raw, scratched, bitten, and frayed at the sleeve.
You and me, together on the lambswool.
All this time, and my chapped lips are still bleeding.
And did we live a lie, apart, not we?
And are we still we, dans la vie démêlé?

Stab Stab Stab

All I really want to do is stab people.
Once, I got a chance to do it.
But the guy kept trying to get away,
and I'd stab him where he was moving.
He'd reach out a hand, a foot, I'd stab it.
After a while, he moved less often,
so I stabbed him a few times in the back.
I talked a little about the woman,
but I wasted the opportunity.
It's just an accident to hack, hack, hack.
To stab, stab, stab is intentional, will.
Resort to speculation is a shame,
but the point, I'd suppose, is intention.

"Step Right Up, Step This Way!"

Is this the exhibit to the conquered?
How much are the tickets to see old friends
chopped to messes, plagued with poxes?
What's the price to see strangers we don't like
crucified on refrigerator doors?
(Which aren't ours, which nobody will touch,
which sanitation just leaves on the corner,
bloody and mildewed, handles gr8y in rust.)
What's it cost extra to kick the sickbed?
Is this where someone else's palsied life
(:"Yes, come one, come all!":) is better left mocked?
Where gumball machines dispense razorblades?
Is this the place for the miracle cure?

Gros Bisous

Maybe you can lie your way out of this. You know I've
always admired your lying. Someone like you doesn't
need to slam doors, or stomp feet, or throw the re-
mote control. Someone like you leaves craters every-
where. Someone like you kicks holes in the sidewalk,
even if her shoes don't fit, even if she runs on the
tippy toes of her claws. You think you haven't tied me
in your hair? Go ahead, just you go ahead and pull.
You can cut through me with ringlets and wire. You
can unspool me in elfin ribbons. But lie to me, liar,
with a French kiss.

Emergency Contact

I've been putting down your number as my emergency contact for a few years, so don't be surprised if you get a call about the demon I summoned and lost, or the memory I had that went rogue and road raged the boardwalk by bumper car. Don't be taken aback by the stranger, so angry, so worried, so familiar, and so knowledgeable about ghost ghosts you gave storm names a long long time ago. And if there never is a voice, email, or FedEx, there's no emergency and I'm just fine, barreling through Luna Park as always, without a care but with a blue Slurpee.

Availability

I understand you're thankful for my help,
that you appreciate all my advice,
which you've always questioned and ignored,
always the same, because you know better.
Once in a while, I was saying to you,
someone volunteers the information
that, as much as they're entitled from you,
you shouldn't expect reciprocation,
and since you do have something to offer,
you will be regularly reminded
to acknowledge your secondary place.
I'd just told you that, when you dropped your pearl.
So, no thanks on the forty minute call.

Old Friend

Applebees and a strip club, all for free.
Isn't that heaven to us, old friend?
Old friend, who stood with me at the divide,
knowing, just briefly, they were just one cliff,
just one crashing chasm of heels and jeans,
and decades, and children who understand.
The children can forgive, unlike the man
who saw the face of Satan in his spleen,
smiling, sanguine, exposed in his white ribs.
If it's not right, what then? If it's not right,
what then? If it's not right, what then? What then?
Heaven is a strip club and Applebees,
and it's all for free, my friend, all for free.

About Me

You said you thought about me this AM.
That would have been right when I was thinking
about how sick I am of this project.
How maybe all I need is a helper
to light it on fire, "the perfect plan."
Every computer, every location,
every page, every last person;
every article and accoutrement
of history, character, or attire:
burn it all. Every single thing gets wicked.
Each one of these thousand sources. Spare nix.
And burn the witnesses, and the witnesses
to the witnesses, greasy as lambs—
so the fire spits and zings in innocence.

The Icing on Top

Right now: the city is white, sick icing
flavored by vermouth and disappointment,
profound, make that profound disappointment;
never never never and nowadays
these skinless skeletons we disgorged,
which was lacerating, I remember,
dance for the coming of the Great Pumpkin,
as if, as if we were still observant,
still believers, still zealots with torches,
or Nike SB Dunk High Pros, or Kool Aid
to give to each other in Dixie cups,
so cherry, cherry, cherry pie flavor.
Maybe, maybe baby. Or maybe just text.

Nekid

We can't hold everything, but we try, all the time, to
hold them longer than we should. Over there in the
windowsill, you'll find a bicycle and sidecar made of
wire, and an oblong beach stone from Havana, as if,
as if, as if I remember, as if I could look back with
these glass eyes. Some stuff, you'll hold as long as you
can stand. That jar, I tried to fill with the river. In this
scar, I would have fossilized fire. But look, I've held
my breath under the ice, and I came in here alone and
nekid, with just my feet, my voice, and my bl8e sky.

"Little Loser"

You would lift me, love me were I less man
than the clenched fist and busted-up bruiser
and tearless deaf-mute Führer that I am.
"Nobody loves me like my little loser."
You would love me if I let the luckless
in; let the little villain believe in
all the trim, TRIBECA wreckers of his
Magoos youth (the couch damask and Georgian);
let the backhand swing and the frying pan
break the window and settle in the trash bags—
two stories thick with tires and old cans—
that's there at the bottom of the airshaft.
"My little loser, you don't ask for much—
just to love me 'til I self-destruct."

New Year's

In spring, sorrow looks through my socket skull
and starlings titter in my deaf ear holes,
and the marsh is most swampy in the bone,
and I feel the sky in a far-off star,
and I taste the black bottom of my jaw.
In summer, I am falling, and digging,
where the ground is soft and the green grass grows,
too grave, from the septic tank to the springhouse.
In autumn, I ride shotgun in the car,
and when I arrive in winter, I saw
through the new sawhorses, burn your sweet home,
and hunt you down while you search for the road.
This year, this year, I resolve to be hell.

"Red Rover, Red Rover"

The iron gate is latched and sealed in black.
And the pigeons coo, nested somewhere close.
Under the saddle swings, the puzzle mats
make pictures of time for each one of us,
and save the grains of sand from the sandpit
to melt down for Champagne flutes and Pentax
lenses—so fine they're radioactive.
The limestone looks over the jungle gym,
and the river knows what the sky tells it,
when they gossip about us and the squirrels,
which isn't something they do all that much
(in a second, no more than a few times).
And voices are crying "here, here" and "home run"
to welcome lost children to the playground.

"Fight You For It"

"I'll fight you for this marble. I'll fight you for this
Dr. Pepper. I'll fight you for this box of tissues and
this boiled egg. I'll fight you for something you lost,
something you really really didn't want to lose. And
maybe baby I won't give it back, even if you beat the
shit out of me, even if I stole it and it was yours, even
if it was brand new, never used. I'll fight you for this
pen without a cap. Hey, hey, hey you. Don't walk away.
Hey. I wanna fight you for this empty keg. Hey you.
Yeah you. You should wanna fight me too."

It's a Nice Day for a

Ride with me, sister, on the bucket seat
when the snow is to-die on the asphalt,
when the sun is #bff to the smog,
and the exhaust has eyes for only us,
and we are broken shark teeth in our row,
rolling from gumline to an open sea,
rolling like the Cuban heels of rockstars
kicking back: velvet couches; and glass ashtrays
on glass coffee tables; and maroon shag
carpets everywhere—everywhere under
our boots and bucket seat and bad radio
and the drub-thrash of the highway at fault.
Ride with me, sister, on the BQE.

Radiant

I'm afraid that child isn't here anymore.
He left on the fog from last February,
taking with him his red fireman hat,
his parents, all torn to rags and once loved,
and two good eyes that were scared of monsters.
Now, from the inside of this gold foil birdcage,
I—as if I, I am I no more—
live as a ground meat burger, without rages,
or a past, or those hundred other doors.
Child, if you come back, bring your baseball glove,
and all three of your red bicycles, and
cut me down if I can't see the sky,
if I can't see that sky again, of ours,
send for your slayers, send for your slayers.

We

We said what we said. Do you remember?
We drank what we drank, and walked where we walked,
and paid who we paid, and saw what we saw,
and took what we took, and lost what we lost,
and talked where we talked, and kept what we kept,
and gave what we gave, and got what we got,
and were what we were, if you remember.
Spearmint mojitos. Mincing stilettos.
Cash on the copper. Disco candelabra.
Bones on the boardwalk. Dulces buenas noches.
Patio table w/ blistered Padrón peppers.
Souvenir pics @Spook-A-Rama, and
a loan against a dollar and a clock.

Everything

There was a time you had everything.
A big, flat glass bowl full of keys and coins.
An old Pentax camera you never used.
A writing desk with plenty of drawers,
made by a carpenter who adored you.
Enough jam jars to serve wine, rum and beer.
A not-so worn out pair of thrift shop jeans.
Two cats: one black, and one white and orange.
Ragg mittens and a red-check duffle coat.
Rubbish and nonsense that stayed at the bar.
Floofy towels and a tub with a view.
A totally foolproof approach to hair.
And the watch I wore and your diamond ring.

At the Tannery

You and I. Then we, on the railroad tracks,
walking the byway, ochre and blue-gray.
Throwing rocks and keeping spikes, nuts and bolts,
wondering what would hold, and what fall apart.
Beyond the houses: the valley, the pond,
the farm, the charred foundations of a school—
and a shimmering mountain of diamonds,
much farther than we thought, and up close, coal.
We climbed from the shade of a mining cart,
hungry for kaeng khiao wan and high voltage
in the bulldozer cab. That end of May.
Once a night, once a day, thunder and clack,
our teeth rat-a-tat as the freight cars passed.

Your Name is Slim, Slim

81

I am more gaunt than my less-than zero,
counted not ghost among the living doomed.
Who but you? Jackdaw, rover, sister?
Slender sickness, me, and we, rotting meat.
Flyer, no flies, from Bangkok, Germany,
or here, where the lies are collected,
hovering at the curbs in white July,
flittering former addresses, texted.
Do you miss the old town, the frozen sleet,
the small white car and bridge on the river?
Your old furniture and organized grooms?
Elysium fields. But not gull, not crow.
Prey above, little sister, or below?

Gum Wrappers

Let's cover the windows with gum wrappers,
and rot a bowl of fruit and watch mold grow
and fruit flies hatch; we'll drain our batteries
and use rolls of aluminum foil
on the antennas and the wireless
so we're shielded from radio waves
and secret transmissions from the others
who might beam in thoughts about not just us,
like nonsense about stuff out there worth saving,
like celebrity gossip and Congress,
like wanted posters and terms of parole.
We won't be subject to frivolities.
You and me and dirty sheets and the glow
of old tv, and fudge pops in the freezer.

Close

83

Tomorrow, tomorrow and tomorrow,
every morning you'll be farther away.
Back when we were kids and you shanked me in
the scrotum with a toenail clipper file,
I wouldn't have believed we'd drift apart.
We really were close, inseparable,
weren't we? And now when you come to town
you email weeks before your arrival
so when you don't text me from the hotel,
the Plaza like old times, I'm sure to know.
Who would have guessed you and I would stay friends?
Laying down our swords and barring our hearts
like prey—and picking up rifles like snipers
and taking aim for the k8llshot, long range.

Caught Looking

You looked at me like I was your maybe
son from this life in another life, or
your father, brother or nearby cousin,
or cousin from far away, or neighbor,
or a stranger you wanted to follow—
to follow right into the afterworld—
where we'd been so close for so long (before),
as mutual collectors of stolen things,
like the size twelve-and-a-half bowling shoe—
Brunswick, just one—from the Pine Street Modell's
by the Kodak place. ("Buy high ISO.")
You looked ... like you had a question for me,
like you knew the answer but might not tell.

Keepers

On Sunday, bring your broken promises,
the two of them, fragrant as tangelos,
and lay them at our two and two tired feet,
and we will see if the floor collapses,
if the world, old as meringue, collapses;
if there are really looking-glass keepers,
who keep watch at the BFF egress;
and we may really hang by our own tresses,
and really, strike the world's red heart with axes,
and really, scream forever and not speak,
and really, swim in a sea of locusts,
on this Sunday, when g8d rests.

Red Balloon

You came around here, quiet and saffron,
and I liked you, and I liked you like that.
You came around here ashen and quirky,
and I liked you, still liked you, just as much.
You came around here, ranting and wretched,
lying and drunken, careless and spiteful,
and asking me to empty my pockets,
my wallet, my calendar, and my veins,
and I liked you, when you asked that I not,
when you put a pin in the blow-up Earth
and the rubber slow-mo'ed the hole, open
for you to rabbit in or rabbit out
to come around or never come again.

Momma

Momma, are there other wooden children?
Momma, am I your only wooden child?
The others, momma, are they more alive?
Do the meat children offer you their hearts?
Momma, you know I have no heart to give,
but I have given you axes, and chainsaws,
and I've said you could cut off my limbs,
you could take me down to timbers, momma.
Chop me down, momma, and I'll give you my stars.
Why momma, why, do I still have my sky?
Oh momma cut me down, or I'll grow wild.
Momma cut me down, if you won't come again,
I have no love, I have no love for the wren.

Curtains

In the bluefire of the television
we watched the whole season and ate ice cream—
covered ourselves in Dulce de Leche,
until the bed was slick and sticky and
goopy and would have to be wadded up,
(us right inside with it), and thrown away.
What a marvelous doomsday that was.
Glory be, those good time armageddons
with space capsules and galactic mishaps
and warp travel accidental—"strap in
for a bumpy ride"—by meteor streams
dismade of onerous physical laws,
and good, so good, for total destruction.

Index

Index of Sequences

John Reed is the author of ten books, including the novels *A Still Small Voice* (Delacorte), *The Whole* (Simon & Schuster/ MTV Books), and the SPD bestseller *Snowball's Chance* (Roof/ Melville House); the definitive non-fiction works *A Drama In Time: The New School Century* (Profile) and *The Never End: The Other Orwell, the Cold War, the CIA, and the Origin of Animal Farm* (Palgrave Macmillan); the play *All The World's A Grave: A New Play By William Shakespeare* (Penguin/Plume); and his highly-praised first collection of sonnets *Free Boat: Collected Lies and Love Poems* (C&R Press). His essay "My Grandma the Poisoner" was selected for *Best American Essays* (Houghton Mifflin). His work has also appeared in publications such as *Tin House, Artforum, Art in America,* the *Los Angeles Times,* the *Paris Review,* the *Times Literary Supplement,* the *Wall Street Journal, The New York Times, Harpers,* and *Rolling Stone.* He holds an MFA in Creative Writing from Columbia University and graduate certificates from Parsons School of Design. He is an Associate Professor and the Director of the MFA in Creative Writing at The New School.

Poems in this sequence were previously published in *Tupelo Quarterly, Shuf Poetry, Silkworm, Schuylkill Valley Journal, Speckled Trout Review, Forever Magazine, Juke Joint, Ink Sac / Cephalo Press, Spilt Milk / Milk Press / PSNY, Smartish Pace, Electric Lit, The Believer, The Denver Quarterly, Vice Magazine, PEN Poetry Series, The Brooklyn Rail, Wordriot, Live Mag!, Rain Taxi, Otter Magazine, Devouring the Green, How Journal, Drift Index, 1AM, Column Collective, Thumbnail Magazine, Intercourse Magazine, Fjords, C&R Press,* and *The Inquisitive Eater.*

9 781963 908770